I0414723

Live And Teach In Vietnam

Peter LeGrove

Find Out About Vietnam So You Have A Better Understanding Of What To Expect Before You Go There

Disclaimer

Although the author and publisher have made every effort to ensure that the information in this book was correct at press time, the author and publisher do not assume and hereby disclaim any liability to any party for any loss, damage, or disruption caused by errors or omissions, whether such errors or omissions result from negligence, accident, or any other cause.

This book is for entertainment purposes only. The views expressed are of the author alone and should not be taken as expert advice. The reader is responsible for his own actions. Neither the author nor the publisher assume any liability or responsibility on behalf of the reader or purchaser of this material.

You must use common sense when traveling in a strange country, The author and publisher assume no liability or responsibility for any accidents or anything that happens to you while reading or following this book. The author is not a licensed Travel Agent in any country in the world, he is an author writing about what he did to find a job in Vietnam.

The author and publisher claim no responsibility for results obtained while following this book, as everybody is different and are starting at different levels. You the reader are responsibility for your actions and safety while trying to teach in Vietnam.

Your Free Book

As a way of saying thank you for buying my book I'm offering you a free book.

This book "How To Add Qualifications To Your CV Using FREE Courses" is about what you can learn over the internet for free. It shows you where to go to get Certificates of Accomplishment that you can add to your CV.

Click here and you will be taken to another page where you can download the free book.

Get Your FREE book here

https://animalsdinosaursandbugs.com/MOOC-download.html

Who Will Benefit From This Book

This book is for anyone who wants to get out there, and see how the other side of the world lives. This book is specific to Vietnam. It will give you an invitation into what to do and what to watch out for, if you want to explore the world teaching English as a Second Language. In most places of the world there are jobs for teachers and Vietnam is one of those places.

This book is for people who want to travel and recent graduates, who with a college degree can get a job in most countries in the world. And why not, if you do not do it for the experience, do it to learn another language. Fluency in another language will put you on the top rung of the corporate ladder. That is if you ever come home.

Vietnam is now a little tiger that is starting to roar, and when countries start to roar English is suddenly in demand. English language teaching is very developed in Vietnam with schools everywhere. But the problem is, how do you get a job with an endless number of teachers, and would be teachers competing for every position available.

Vietnam is a good country for teaching but now it has reduced its visa to 30 days. China is down to a one month visa, and in Thailand some people only get two months. Hong Kong still has the 3 month visa at the airport but for how long. That is one reason there are a lot of teachers here. As the countries modernize the visa requirements get more stringent.

If you are on the lookout for a country where you can "Live Cheap In An UnCheap World" then put Vietnam on your radar. Then go there and get a job teaching.

How To Use This Book

This book is an introduction into teaching ESL in Vietnam. Check out the links and see what they have to offer. The internet is information, use it. Look at the job sites and see what is available. See which jobs you would like to do, and see what you need to have to be able to apply for the job. Then get on the internet to perfect your craft. You cannot expect to teach a class of kids, if you have never taught before.

Also the book goes into depth about living in Vietnam and what you are up against. So plan ahead about how you will survive. Vietnam is a great country to teach in, but there are traps you have to be aware of. And it is up to you to make sure you do not fall into them. The book is about making your stay in Vietnam, an enjoyable experience.

Vietnam is developing, but not as fast as China, and they still have the rip off mentality. In a lot of cases you are just a cash cow to be milked, and this book tries to point you in a different direction, where you can arrange your life around modern technology. With a smart phone and a few select apps, your experience in Vietnam should be a lot better. And you shouldn't get ripped off as often.

Read the book, check out the websites, look up the facebook pages and download the apps you will need, and learn how to use them. To minimize getting ripped off, use Grab, and have your currency converter available as well as maps.me. When you first arrive in Vietnam, try and get a sim card and a phone package as soon as possible. Once you are back online life is back to normal.

What Is In This Book

Update After Covid

Vietnam has changed dramatically since before covid. But I must admit it was starting to change just as covid came along and now since they've had two years of lockdown the teaching situation has changed. Basically all kids attended zoom school for nearly a year and before they were allowed back in the classroom they all had to be vaccinated twice. I don't know the vaccine rollout figures for Vietnam but a lot of people in the cities were vaccinated. I have no idea what the vaccination rate was like in the countryside. Also some job advertisements say you have to be double vaxxed to get the job. At the moment that seems to apply to the large companies even though it has been said that that is a requirement of the government. If you are not into American Pharmaceutical companies you should be able to pick up the Russian or Chinese vax somewhere if you do need to be vaxxed.

Now at the end of May 2022 the country is nearly completely opened up. At the moment you can fly in whether you're vaccinated or unvaccinated, you do not need a covid test and you still don't need a return ticket. But and this is a very big but, the visa on arrival VOA is no more. All you can get now to enter the country is a 1 months e-visa that at the moment is not renewable in the country. So you still have to do your visa runs every month, not every three months like before. It's not so bad when you live in HCMC as you can run the border into Cambodia and back in a day. At the moment all you have to do is leave Vietnam when you're e-visa either runs out or before and re-enter on another e-visa. All you have to do is make sure you apply for your e visa at least 2 weeks before you leave to get back in the country again. It can take up to 2 weeks to get your e-visa so make sure you apply early. That even applies before you leave your home country to go to Vietnam. They say it takes 3 days on the website.

In Hanoi if you're doing a visa run by bus to Laos it takes 2 days or one night and 2 days or you can fly to Laos or Cambodia and then fly back in again to Vietnam. As with all travel now you must check the covid requirements of the country you are going to and they change all the time. Also if you are living in a Transit Lounge check the covid regulations and how long you can stay there, usually 24 hours.

It is economically not a good idea to have to fly to another country to get a visa for one month. But if you are going to apply for a work permit or some other permit you need to have your University papers all apostilled in your home country before you leave to go to Vietnam. The standard certified copy is no longer acceptable. At the moment because it is all new and the border has just opened up we are not sure of any shortcuts yet.

With these new changes I am taking Vietnam off my list of places to go too which is a pity cos I like it here, but doing visa runs every month makes it uneconomical to live there unless you live in HCMC and not Hanoi where I like to live.

During covid I was teaching my students in Hanoi online using the standard Google Meet, but as school has gone back now most students are just sick and tired of online learning and they want the classroom, so my online learning classes just collapsed. Anyway school finishes soon so I hope to pickup some summer classes and then re decide what to do about my Vietnam lifestyle. I will probably check out Cambodia and Laos and see what it's like there as I do like living in Southeast Asia.

Now with the world heading into famine and food shortages I am trying to find a country that will not be so affected by what's going to happen in the future, which could also mean nuclear war but I hope not.

At the moment the Laos border is open to vaccinated individuals and anyone not fully vaccinated or unvaxxed needs the rapid antigen test within 48 hours of going there. In Cambodia it is slightly different, if you're unvaxxed you need to quarantine for 7 days. So if you're fully vaxxed you'll have no problem running for visas in either of those two places. Anything to do with covid travel restrictions and whatever in any country can change at any time so keep abreast of everything or you might not get in.

China is a standard disaster and the covid regulations are changing regularly and so are visas and whatever. I still don't know how I managed to live there for so long but now I don't think I can get back in again. Last time I tried to get back into China was during the Hong Kong riots not a good time to travel. Anyway I never got back to China, it was easier to get a flight out of Hong Kong and even that was difficult with the airport surrounded by protesters. So travelling during these difficult times could either be exciting or a disaster depending on what happens.

When you are planning to come to Hanoi there are two types of information on the internet. One is pre covid which is basically all wrong and scattered between all wrong stuff you might find some right stuff but it's very hard to find. So expect everything you see or read on the internet to be incorrect and you might get somewhere. I actually think Hanoi is better than before, the traffic is not as bad and the motorcycle taxis even though there are less, they are still just as bad. Before Grab motorbikes were everywhere and the drivers uniforms were clean and they had two lids. Now the uniforms are all faded and they have devolved back to what the motorcycle taxis were like before Grab came along, except now Grab are all the old motorcycle taxis reincarnated. I downloaded the app because to survive in this city you need the app. When you arrive here at all the bus stations you will be inundated with all these motorcycle taxi drivers dressed in old faded Grab gear and they will call themselves motorcycle taxis not Grab. The real grab drivers wear spotless uniforms and have clean bikes and two grab helmets. The problem with the Grab app is they always ring you before they find you and when they hear you speaking English they don't come and you have to start the process all over again, so it is better to have a friend who speaks Vietnamese around and that way you should get a ride. I always use the grab app for cars but I've always heard a Vietnamese speaker directing the driver to help find me. In Hanoi a licensed Grab driver is a friend if you can get one that speaks English you got a friend for life but they are few and far between.

Also the old hostels and hotels that used to be the most popular places on the planet have all changed hands or are boarded up. I managed to end up in an illegal hotel that I walked past many times before when I lived here. If you are returning assume nothing is the same and you'll be OK. If you are new to here you will love it as it is still the same but the atmosphere has changed.

One thing you have to be careful of is while we were all Locked down and hiding under the pillows and whatever, Google, Microsoft and Amazon and who ever else is trying to run the internet was working overtime. And you don't find that out until you end up in a country away from your home country. so far I've been locked out of facebook and I have to use my google password to open up my saved passwords folder to find the passwords that I need. If you are my age you'll understand what "Catch 22" means so before you leave invest in a cheap VPN that you can set to you home country and that way the alphabet soup still thinks you are at home and hopefully wont lock you out of anything. And you need the VPN when you access your bank or they wont let you in. Make sure you access your bank when it is open in your home country time. Another very important part of travelling that you have to keep on top of is when your cards from the bank expire. It's not so bad in your home country as you can race down the bank and get another one but when your bank is a couple of flights away it makes it slightly more difficult. Another part of keeping safe online when accessing your bank is when the bank sends you a code on your mobile phone that you have to enter into your transaction for it to go through. I asked my bank about how I can stop them and they said you can't, and I walked out of the bank mumbling obscenities under my breath. Hopefully the bank app should work without too many problems I hope. But just in case I managed to get a chunk of US dollars from the local currency exchange as the banks don't exchange currency anymore. I got small bills under $100 having big bills can cause a problem when you are changing them over.

Now this bank thing is a problem and it will cause problems. When I went to renew my visa I didn't turn on my VPN and the bank sent me a message saying they had sent my phone a text and I was to type in the number for the payment to go through. Well I couldn't, my home phone was sitting on the kitchen table at home so my daughter couldn't send me the text or the number. Anyway when I realized my VPN was not on I switched it on and re-did the whole thing again and because the fee for the visa was only $25 it went through. I'm not sure what the cutoff amount of money is for the bank to not send a text but I'm sure it's not high enough to buy plane tickets. I have to arrange something with my daughter to sort something out every time I need to buy a plane ticket and that could be a serious problem in itself. So to sum up modern technology is an advantage but when you are on holiday in a country far far away it suddenly turns into a serious disadvantage.

Hanoi used to be the place because of the 3-month Visa, now with only a one month Visa it is not really the place. Most teaching contracts at schools are one year or even two years. So if you are just after three months work for the summer, forget it. At the moment after a month you have to run to Laos, Cambodia or even Thailand to renew your Visa. So that means your first four or five lessons are to pay for your Visa and all the rest after that pay for your rent, food and entertainment. And what is left over you save hopefully. If you get a year contract with a school you will be sitting pretty. You will be living in one of the best countries in the world and in one of the best cities, surrounded by friendly people and cheap food, booze and cigarettes if you smoke. So I think the best thing to do is to plan to stay here for a year, so get all your papers in order before you come over here and that usually means they have to be approved by your government before you can apply for a work visa.

Who I Am And What I Do

Hi. My name is Peter LeGrove, and I'm here to tell you my boots on the ground experience, about what it's like to get a job teaching English in Vietnam. I did it and it isn't easy, so I'll try to make it easier for you. Now I have spent most of my life travelling around the globe teaching English. From Mexico to Indonesia then onto China via Hong Kong. And the biggest change over the last few years, is how countries have tightened up on visas, and how long you can stay inside the country. Only a few years ago in Vietnam, all you needed to do was leave the country and come back in again for another three months. Now you have to leave the country, get a visa and come back in again. Or leave, get an online visa or Visa on Arrival and fly back in again. You are looking at between $100 to $300 US just for flights every three months just to get a visa and then there is the visa cost. The Visa on Arrival letter that you need to have to get on a plane usually cost $15 to $20 US dollars and then at the airport you have to pay another $25 to $50 to get the visa. Or you can get a Business Visa for 6 months if you want and the price is not cheap. It cost $95 US to get the Visa on Arrival Letter and then you have to pay around $320 for the service fee so forget it. Also there have been problems with the business visa so to be safe stick with the tourist visa. So the days of running round the globe on cheap visas, are getting less and less. But in South East Asia there are still a few more countries to go to.

Gone are the days in China, where we used to run the border to Hong Kong, to get another three month visa. Now it is 30 days and that is all you get. So teaching in China has taken a nose dive, and I think that is why there are so many teachers here in Vietnam. It is one of the last countries to get a three month visa. And they are not cheap. It cost me 600 RMB yuan, at the Vietnam Embassy in Guangzhou China, to get a three month visa.

Even Thailand has tightened up, and a number of teachers have relocated here to Vietnam, where it is still possible to get a three month visa, or longer if you get a business visa but they are starting to get pricey. Anyway the schools in Vietnam are used to the teachers taking off for a visa run so it is no real problem. Things in Vietnam are pretty relaxed. Anyway as of March 2019 the 6 month and 1 year business visa were only available to USA passports so stick with the tried and true visa run and have a weekend in Thailand.

Now it is time to sit back and relax, to find out how easy, or how difficult it is to get a job teaching English in Vietnam. Nowadays with the internet, smart phones and Google Play, your world of travelling is a lot easier. But you have to keep up to date with the apps, as new ones are coming out all the time. Like maps.me which is run of GPS not data, so you can still find your way around, as soon as you land in Vietnam or any other country.

This Is How I Did It And What I Learned

Vietnam is a tourist Mecca, with tourists crawling all over the cities and countryside. The whole of the Hanoi old quarter is full of hostels and hotels,that cater to all levels of expense. From the cheapest hostel at $3.50 per night, to upwards of whatever you can afford or want to pay. And the whole country is geared for the tourists, with organized tours to where ever you want to go. And dispersed amongst the tourists are the semi permanent foreign workers, mainly teachers, etching out a living in this beautiful country, with a fair bit of pollution in the main cities, but not as bad as China. It seems the whole teaching system here is, basically going from one school to another. Most teachers ride motorbikes or use Grab which is easier because you do not need to know where you are going and sometimes the Grab drivers get lost. And the teachers come and go like flies. I met an American teacher who has been here for over 8 years. And he still didn't know if he was going to stay any longer. He just went from one visa run to another. And I'd say a lot of teachers are the same. The last visa run, turns into an exit to Thailand or China or some place else.

In the main cities the competition for jobs is fairly intense, but out of the cities they are always on the lookout for teachers. And some teachers come here with hopes of getting a job, and end up in Cambodia, where it is easier to get a job. Some people come here and crash out on a beach, and just give up looking for jobs. Life in good here. It comes under "How To Live Cheap In An UnCheap World." And out of the tourist places and big cities, it is still cheap with beautiful beaches. And the joy of modernization is, you can crash out on an idyllic beach, and teach kids in China over the internet. You are not confined to the four walls of a classroom. And if you love beaches, sun, sand and a few beers after work, then this is the country to crash out in.

I have to say it but Vietnam is the place, as you can still get a three month visa. China was the place but now Vietnam is the place. Hong Kong used to be place before the Handover, but it has stayed the same, we could call Hong Kong the baseline. Before, like about 15 to 20 years ago, when you went from Hong Kong into China you went back in time, like about back to the 30s. Now when you go across the border at Lowu you are going into 2030, that's how advanced China has become in the last 20 years. But some things never change and Hong Kong is one of them. Most countries can still get a 30 day visa at the border in Hong Kong, just check to make sure you have visa free entry. It is now the same in China, they usually only give you 30 days in the country, and you still have to get a very expensive visa. A far cry from the three month visas we used to get a couple of years back that cost next to nothing. As economies around the world are having problems, the visa restrictions are loosening up, but not so in Asia where some economies are booming. In the big cities in China there is a sea of people just spending money and that is what keeps the economy going. When economies start slipping back into a recession or an economic downturn, they tend to live off tourists, and to get tourists they make it easier to get into the country.

One thing I did that I highly recommend is join https://www.italki.com/ and find some language partners and hopefully you will have friends here when you get here. Anyway that is what I did and I still have coffee with a friend I met on italki, now 6 years later.

Welcome To Hanoi

Hanoi is a standard rip off tourist city, so get used to it. Taxis are notorious as well as motorcycle taxis, so expect to get ripped off. The taxi fare from the airport is $18US that is a fixed price. In the city if you flag down a taxi you should be on the meter, but some meters have been tampered with. I stick to Grab motorbike taxi, they are slightly more honest than most. If a taxi driver gives you a price on his phone or something, just get out you are dealing with a rip off merchant.

Getting from the airport to Hoan Kiem Lake where everybody goes, can get expensive. But there are some cheaper options, like the Orange bus number 86 that costs 35.000 dong (local money). The last stop of this bus is the Train Station in Hoan Kiem, but you should get off before that. Either the first stop in Hoan Kiem which is Long Bien Bus Station, or the second stop which is smack bang in the old quarter, where hostels and hotels are everywhere. But it is on the wrong side of the lake, so you are up for a 20 minute walk to get to the Cathedral. Taxis range in price from $20 US down to $15 if you walk around the airport looking lost long enough. Get the price before you get into a taxi, they are thieves so are the motorbike taxies. Always get the price first. In the city the taxies use the meter so it is not so bad. Never get on a motorbike taxi without getting the price first. Grab always gives you a price first. The Grab drivers all wear a green jacket. It is all done on your smart phone, you just have to install the app. It should be on Google Play Store. If you are dealing with an ordinary motorcycle taxi I usually hand them my little notebook so they can write the price down. There is a difference in the sound of 15 and 50 so get used to it. Grab is the way to go until you rent yourself a motorbike. I use Grab nearly every day. I usually take the bus to the nearest stop then get a Grab to take me to the school. This is easier and it saves time and a lot of walking time.

In Hoan Kiem there are lots of hostels, ranging in price from the cheapest around $3.50 US to whatever you want to pay. If you can't find a cheap place to stay, just book for one night and look around further. If you are getting a room, check them out, and that could mean walking around a number of different hostels. If you are with friends, park in a cafe, and all leave your bags there with one person and the rest can go looking around. Do not get lost. The price range is basically the same, but the quality can change dramatically. One hotel charged $13 for a very basic room, whereas you could pick up a luxury room for $15, in a hotel around the corner. Hostels are the same, for $5 you can get a really lively hostel while another place is a dump. I stayed in one hostel for $4 and it was really good except the people there were very unfriendly. If they were more friendly it would have been the best place I stayed but it was not to be. Another hostel was only $3 and it had a free keg you could drink as much as you liked. And it was a good hostel, so it varies. Just check out a few before you settle into one place.

Hanoi is a city that has been left behind. The buildings look the same, but the signs have changed. Mainly into hotel and hostel signs and they are everywhere, so you should have no problem getting a place to stay. Motorbikes, cars and crossing the road is a problem, but you get used to it. Mainly because you have too. The best way to cross the road is slowly, and that gives them time to see you, slow down and ride around you. Now I just keep an eye on the cars, as the bikes are everywhere. The golden rule for crossing the road is always go forward never go back. The drivers all expect you to go forward.

This is a standard Asia city, so you are going to get ripped off the first day or two. If you can find a VinMart shop or a supermarket, the prices are fixed and very reasonable. They are the Hanoi version of the 7-11, and they are changing the pricing of the street merchants. You must bargain with the street merchants, as they will give you an inflated price. Food is pretty cheap on the street, but it can get pricey in the restaurants.

Load Up On Some Apps

Now make sure you can get these apps on your phone, Google maps, Google Translate or another translator, and a currency converter. And to get around this city you need Grab, so download these apps. This way you only need to know where you want to go, not how to get there. Which is a plus, as this city is a disaster to get around. If you want to buy or rent a motorbike, you can, but then you have to learn how to get around this city. With these two apps, all you need to know is where you want to go, and not how to get there. With Grab the rides average at about 5000 dong / kilometer, and it comes out of your account or you can pay cash. The motorbike taxies usually charge as much as they can get, but that is a dying job, so using Grab can save you some money and piece of mind. I use Grab whenever I can but away from the city center Grab is very hard to get, as they ring you first and when they hear a foreigner some don't show up. Grab is a better option in the city center so away from the center get your school to get a Grab and they can talk to the driver. With Grab the price usually comes up before you leave, and in most cases that is what you pay.

When you use Google Maps use you GPS, so you know where you are, because if you do not know where you are, how do you find out where you are going. Google Maps make life easy. Now with Google Translate, China has this under control. When you walk into a shop, someone will stick a phone under your nose, and you write down in English what you want, and up comes the Chinese and they go and get it for you. All under control, they have mastered technology. But here in Hanoi they are still a long way behind, and you have to use your translator on your phone. Next up the currency converter comes into play, so you know how much you are paying. Then you can bargain using the converter if you like. In the markets you can drop the price a lot, but in the shops it is different, and if the price is marked forget it, it doesn't change. Now to get all these to work you need a sim card and a data pack. If you want to get minutes on your phone they charge you 2000Dong /minute. I got 70 minutes for 140,000Dong plus a data pack for 70,000Dong. And nobody seems to know how long it lasts. Some say when it runs out just top it up, and others say you have to use it up. This is the standard tourist pack that most shops sell. It is reasonably cheap, but you probably wont use it all up very fast, but to get a job you need a phone number. Also you need an address, so don't say you live in a hotel, just give the street address if asked.

Here It Is – Getting A Teaching Job

Now to get a job in Vietnam, especially in Hanoi, is the same as getting a job anywhere. So have a really good CV and a really decent cover letter, that you write for each job. Also tailor you CV to suit the job. You really need three different CV's. One for kids, another for adults and IELTS, and one with a mixture for both kids and adults. And send the right CV to the appropriate jobs. If they are looking for a children's teacher, send the CV for children etc etc. Now on the cover letter, don't put anything that will stop them from opening your CV. You must realize with some jobs there are heaps of people applying, especially for the good daytime, full-time jobs. Most jobs are evening and weekend English schools for kids, with a few adult schools thrown in. So evening schools are the easiest jobs to get, but they don't have too many hours. And they like to have a number of foreigners working for them, so if one takes the day off, someone else can fill in. That is why you need to work at a number of different schools, and that is where Grab comes in, so get the app. With Grab you do not need to learn your way around this city, which is a plus, and they are quite reasonable.

Also if you get a room out of the city center print out your CV and drop it off at any school within walking distance. Doing this has landed many a teacher a job or two. There are schools tucked away in some very out of the way places, and there are small English centers and kindergartens scattered through out this city.

On Google Maps the bus numbers come up, so if you are into buses, then try it out. The buses usually cost 7000 dong a ride. You get on, then the conductor will collect your money and give you a ticket. So get a seat first then the conductor will come to you. During rush hour the buses are a bit slow, but usually they are pretty good. Finding a direct bus is not a problem, all you have to do is look at the bus numbers where you want to go, and try and find one that matches up near where you live. Most people ride motorbikes, so they don't know the buses. Students have a bus pass, so they do know the buses. If you have any problems ask a student. But most do not understand English, and they sometimes go and find one of there classmates, who does understand English, so they can be helpful. Also on the bus, you can show the bus conductor on the map where you want to go, and hopefully they should tell you where to get off, but not always the case as I found out the hard way.

In Hanoi the complete address, the number and the street name, is written on the shop frontage, so you always know where you are. Comes in handy when you are using Grab. But on the buses it makes life a lot easier. When you know where you are going, write down the street names, then look out the bus window to see where you are. Also you can use Google on topography to see the parks or whatever, or you can use street view. But that doesn't work because everything looks the same. I would recommend you write down the address of the school you are going to, and how to get there. Like all the directions, turn right on this street and then turn left on this street, and write down the name of the street. So you can follow it on your phone. Then if you get lost, call Grab and they'll take you there, but it is 10000 dong minimum, so if you only go around the corner you still have to pay 10000 dong. As I had to once. If I had written down the address, and how to get there I would have been all right. Google directions got it wrong so don't trust Google all the time. Once an Grab driver got lost, and that was because Google didn't know where to go. That was my most expensive Grab trip to date.

Now back to buses, Because of the one way system in Hanoi, the bus usually comes back on another road, so make sure you have GPS enabled, so you can get off the bus reasonable close to where you live. It can be quite daunting getting lost on the buses after class, on the way home from school after 9 pm at night. Also sometimes the last bus is at 9 pm. Just be careful relying on the GPS on your phone because if you lose your phone or it is stolen you wont know where you are or how to get back to your hotel. I use the GPS when I am really lost and don't know where I am, let alone where I am going.

Now for Vietnam there are a number of Facebook groups like Hanoi Massive Jobs, https://www.facebook.com/groups/hanoimassivejobs/ Hanoi English Teaching Jobs - https://www.facebook.com/groups/ 1517310348497729/ They are all very good with jobs being added every day, and if you want to do relief teaching, Facebook groups are the places to go. If you want to leave your job and you need to replace yourself, then this is where you go to get a teacher. If you are a teacher, you can advertise yourself here. Because it is free, be careful of scams, so use your common sense. Sometimes you see a job, and in the comments people who are not happy with the company say so, especially if they don't get paid. There is one big problem here, and that is you get paid monthly, same in most of Asia. So if you are running out of money, ask and see if you can get some. When I was teaching part time I asked to get paid after class or weekly. If they still wanted to pay monthly I would leave. If you only work one day a week, then why wait a month to get paid. A lot of small schools would pay after class, but the big school companies paid monthly. I ended up with half paying after class, and the big companies paying monthly. This way I always had cash. If you are a bit tight for cash, go relief teaching you get paid after the class, but they are very hard to get. They all advertise on the Facebook groups.

Now for around the country you can have a look at these groups

https://www.facebook.com/teachingjobsinVienam2016/

https://www.facebook.com/VietNamteachingJobsdotcom/

https://www.facebook.com/TeachinVN/

and for Saigon look at this site

https://www.facebook.com/groups/1521862661370506/

Now you must be careful as some schools are, to say the least, not very honest. So do a facebook page search using the name of the school and see what pops up. Use control f (standard page search command) to get a search box at the bottom left corner of the page, and type in what you are looking for. Then click through them all and see how bad or good things are. When you follow the facebook pages for jobs, you will see some pretty nasty stuff can happen, and there is very little you can do about it, except warn other people.

How To Get Started Finding A Job

When you first come here to teach, tell everybody you know at the dorm, that you are a teacher looking for a job, and somebody might know somebody etc etc and this is possibly the best way to get a job. When I was leaving I tried to replace myself this way, and I couldn't get anybody to take over my jobs. The two people I approached were just not interested even though they needed the money. And these jobs paid after class. You could even get some business cards printed and hand them out. Make sure they have your photo on them so people can see what you look like.

Facebook groups seem to have taken over, so if you want to find anything just search facebook and see what is out there like Hanoi Comrades https://www.facebook.com/groups/581773388574145/

Now to get a work visa you need a degree, an English Teaching certificate, and a police clearance letter, which you have to get from a government department in your country. Then you have to get it notarized and apostilled (legalized/ authenticated) at another government department, which is one big hassle. In my country it takes about a month to get the police clearance letter, and then another couple of weeks to get it apostilled and that costs more than a few dollars. So if you are serious then get it done, but most English schools don't ask. If you live in Vietnam more that 6 months you can get a police clearance letter here and they will accept that. I think all your documents have to be notarized and apostilled in your country. So it is a bit of a hassle getting a work permit, and you usually have to survive on going on a visa run every three months, to get another visa to stay here.

At the moment the visa rules are changing nearly every month, so it is hard to keep up to date on the changes. After President Obama visited Vietnam, an agreement was reached where American passports could get a one year multi entry visa. I don't know how much that will cost but that is a good deal. Americans will not need to go on a visa run but I think they can only stay in Vietnam for 3 then they have to leave the country and come back in again. Projecting forward, I would say that would make Americans the most sort after teachers, as they can stay here the longest.

Visa Runs

Update 2022 My First Visa Run

My 30-day tourist visa was running out so I setup a Visa Run to Thailand. Back in the day before covid when we did a Visa Run every 3 months it was no problem. Now a visa run every month is causing me to rethink how I will stay here. Most teaching contacts are either one year and they are actually bringing in a 2 year contract. Before most schools relied on teachers doing a 3-month Visa run. Now they are having to rethink the situation.

Anyway the Thailand Visa Run is still available where you fly into Thailand in the morning and fly out in the afternoon. Thailand his two airports and usually you fly into one and have to fly out the other. To transfer between the airports there is a free shuttle bus. The shuttle bus is easy to find it's on Level 2 Gate 3. Just walk out the gate across a few roads and you'll see the shuttle bus stop on your right. You will need to have a ticket leaving the airport you're going too or you will have to pay I think. I showed my passport and my ticket and they gave me a ticket to get on the bus. Everything went okay at the airport it was no problem and I got there at a slow time so I just walked straight through.

I actually made more mistakes back in Hanoi then I did in Thailand. The city bus from the airport to the city center is bus number 86. It has always been bus number 86 but since covid they have added another bus, bus number 68 that takes you to another part of the city. Now these buses are the same color, same everything except the number, and I got on the wrong bus. I was lucky the bus driver asked me where I was going and kicked me off and told me to get the other bus. Usually incidents like that are not a problem but the last bus leaves at 9:40 and this was the last bus. The only problem with the Visa Run was there is only one evening flight and that gets in at 8:30 leaving you one hour to get through immigration, get your bags and get the bus. A very tight schedule so if you miss the last bus you're looking at a million dong for a taxi as opposed to 45 dong for the bus.

A Visa Run every month makes it nearly unprofitable to work here and do Visa runs like before. Unless you live in Ho Chi Minh City where it's easy to run the border to Laos and doesn't take very long. Doing an overland border run from Hanoi usually takes two days. So now if you really love the city it's time to get a school to sponsor you so you can get a one year visa and then you can get the Temporary Resident Permit and stay here for a year or longer. I like the city, I like the country, and I like the jobs and the people and the kids but I also like traveling and moving around that is why I don't want to get the one year visa. And now if the war between Russia and America doesn't happen there is a lot of countries over there I want to visit and they still have 3 months, 6 months and up to 1 year visa on Entry at the airport. So countries like Vietnam and other Southeast Asia countries that restrict tourism or restrict people from living there they will be left out of The Best Places To Live And Work In List in 2023.

Visa Run Pre-covid

The general consensus on visas is, to extend a three month visa you have to leave the country as there were a lot of fake visa stamps around. Also they try to get you to get a business visa, and this can be very expensive. So only get a business visa if you intend to stay here for a while. If not work illegally on a tourist visa, but you can get deported and fined if you get caught working. It does happen from time to time. Just before your visa is about to expire, ask around and somebody will tell you about a good agent, who will get you a decent visa run price. Usually that entails a return ticket out of the country, with a letter allowing you to get a visa at the airport, on your way back into Vietnam.

Now there seems to be a bit of a grey area to do with part time work. And the general understanding is, you basically can work part time but it is still illegal. So most schools only hire part time workers. So you have to keep applying for any jobs that you can do, and more importantly you can get to. A number of teachers I met are on a business visa but at the moment business visas are not stable so stick to a tourist visa. At the moment the only way to extend your visa, is to do a visa run to Bangkok, Thailand, where you can either stay the night, or change airports to fly back to Vietnam again. If you want to hang around in South East Asia, then shoot into Cambodia for a quick look at Angkor Wat, while you are waiting for your visa, which typically takes 3 days to get. Then head into Laos for a quick look. You will have to check your visa requirements for other South East Asia countries, depending on which country you are from.

Teaching in Vietnam can be a big hassle. So you need to get the hours to make it worth while to stay here. And it seems the turnover in teachers is quite high. So the bottom line is keep applying for jobs. It's a numbers game, the more you apply for the sooner you will get something.

There is a serious problem with foreign teachers coming and going. It boils down to basically if you can't get the hours or enough hours to cover your living expenses and visa runs, and unless you fall in love, there is really no reason to stay here. And that is the situation at the moment. Even teachers with good jobs and good living conditions leave. They just can't hack the heat, or the traffic, or the constant hassle of living here, so they up and leave. Just check out the classified section and see people trying to sell out so they can leave. I once saw a gym membership going for pennies on the dollar. Motorbikes are always for sale, and you should be able to pick up a bargain very easily. But foreigners are a picky bunch, and they would rather not sell a cheap bike to you, but sell it to a bike shop for less. In one dorm when these guys were leaving they said, "Who wants my bike. Take me to the airport and it is yours" And one of the other travellers got a free bike, but to my knowledge, that doesn't happen very often.

You can do your own visa run yourself buying online but the biggest hassle is getting things printed, and you need the Visa On Entry papers printed out as well as you air tickets. I ask at the school and they usually print for me. There are print shops around but they like just photocopying things. You need to put the documents on a usb stick and then take them into the shop. If you get an agent to do it you don't have to worry about getting things printed. Also the agents know that you live in Vietnam so they are very reasonable.

There are many places where you can get the Visa On Entry for around $17 US I use this place they are pretty good http://vietnamvisapro.net/ I had no problems I filled out the form sent the money then printed off the Entry Visa. At the airport when you get here you just stand in line at the counter will all the other foreigners, hand in your passport and the Visa documents then they call you name using Google speech and you hand over one photo and $25 US, If you do not have a photo that will cost you another $1. Very straight forward nothing to worry about.

My Breakdown Of Costs Per Month

First 5 lessons for visa. The visa run usually costs $300 so that is $100 each month

Accommodation 7 to 10 lessons that is about $200 per month for a room or $150 in a dorm.

Return plane ticket to your home country about 50 lessons for me, over the whole time you are there. Say 20 lessons each month for the first visa run.

Then comes living expenses. Vietnam is pretty cheap if you don't get ripped off too much. Say 5 lessons.

Your entertainment expenses are up to you, another 5 lessons.

Saving what is left.

That is all up about 45 lessons for 3 months. Usually you work about 20 lessons a month, so you can see you have to stay longer than one visa run to break even.

Also don't expect to land your first job the first week you are there. It can take a while of constantly sending out your CV.

At the end of the day you do save money, but the first 3 months is just cost recovery months, after that you start to make some money. So plan on doing at least one visa run to break even. Now you will be better off applying for jobs out of the city. They usually come with accommodation, so that is one less part of living in Vietnam that you do not need to worry about. Sometimes the pay is less but the cost of living is also less. So you win again. You will have more chance of getting a job if you live away from the city.

Applying For Jobs

You can assume when you apply for a job, so do a lot of other people and they do. You just need to see the comments on Massive, from the people who have already applied for the job. That is what you are up against. So your cover letter must attract the attention of the person looking at your CV, or it will just get deleted. I would say, anything in the cover letter that they don't like will get it deleted. Make sure you give them everything they ask for. Also your facebook page might get looked at, so don't have anything that could work against you, front and center on your facebook page. Also schools look at Massive to pick up teachers. So you can advertise yourself on Massive and see what happens. Anyway if you do, you will see that the school looking for a teacher answers all the advertisements, so you are still up against the numbers. Also if you apply for a job and leave a message saying you have sent an email or something, you could be contacted by someone looking for a teacher. As they say nothing is private on Facebook. Anyway, after you have been to a few interviews, you soon know whether you are going to get the job or not, or whether you want the job or not. I had to give a demo class at one agent, and he had already picked who was going to get the job. So you get the feelings or the vibes. And the standard rules apply, if any parent complains about you, like your accent or you talk too fast, you are gone.

You will notice that some advertisements appear over and over again. So I think the school must look at a few applicants, pick one then delete the rest. So keep applying to the same schools, over and over again until you get a job. I applied for some jobs, had an interview then turned down the job. If for some reason I didn't like the location, or the company, or whatever, I would send an email declining the job and give a reason. I declined one job because they didn't pay for the demo class. If you do a full lesson most schools will pay you for the lesson. If you do a demo class in the office in front of the staff, you will not get paid.

When you see a job you would like to apply for - I would first find the address on Google maps, to find out if I could get to it with Grab or which buses I need. On Google maps, I would use the Directions function to find out which buses to use, or if I could walk there. Now Google does screw up, so check other available routes. If I couldn't get to the school for some reason or another, I would forget it and try another one. For me the most important thing was being able to get to the school easily. If you use the buses, they do not go everywhere and you could be up for a 20 minute walk in some cases. Also some buses stop running at

9 0'clock, so you might have to get Grab or a taxi. If I got Grab I would go home, but if I got a taxi I would only go to another bus stop. And if you are a long way from the city center there is no Grab, it is just too far away and there are no drivers out there. Then again Grab seems to have bikes everywhere so you should be able to pick one of those.

Also make sure you know how many hours you will be working. One school started off by saying two hours, then it got down to one hour for you and one hour for the Vietnamese teacher. Then they said they would send an email to let me know if I had the job. And I said don't bother. A lot of classes are only for one hour, so I would politely refuse. Don't get locked into any one hour classes unless you have a motorbike and can get to your next class. Or you could be stuck doing a one hour class in the evening, when you should be getting 2 or 3 hours. In some kindergartens they have half hour classes, so be careful what you are getting yourself into. Do not be afraid to turn down a class, if it is in the wrong place or the hours are no good. I was lucky at one demo class, one parent complained about my accent so I never got the job. I was very lucky as it was a new school and they said they would have more classes, but three months later they were still advertising for one hour a night.

Also usually I wanted to get paid weekly or after class, not monthly for part time work. For full time getting paid monthly is usual, but I would not do that for part time. It looks like I am pretty picky but it pays off in the long run. So don't get into a situation where you need money. If you are running out of money, apply for jobs out of the city where you get a decent wage at one job and usually accommodation supplied. If you don't need to live in the city, don't, you can make more money and have more fun living in the county side. Also if you live in the backpackers or a hotel they can hold your passport, so you can owe money on your rent until you get paid.

I did get hooked up into one situation with two small schools. I was working for one school and it was quite good, and I found out later they had a second school on the outskirts of the city. And they wanted me to go out there to do some classes. I basically had too as I was already working for this other school. The classes were good, the kids were good, the teaching assistants were good but it was over an hour and a half to get there, two buses and I was stuck out in the middle of the rice paddies. And the class was only for an hour and they paid below the usual wage. So be careful when you go for jobs.

Also during term time you can get a job at the public schools as a teacher. Now to get these jobs you usually go through an agent. There are many advertising on the TNH website, and I honestly can't tell you which is the best agent. There are enough stories on the Massive jobs website to put you off the lot, but it is work. So take your pick and see what happens. With this type of work you could end up running all over the city. Some ask you to have a motorbike so you can go to more schools. Just don't kill yourself travelling all over the city. It could be 40 minutes in a classroom and 40 minutes to get to the next class. Use Grab they will save you a lot of time.

What To Do For Accommodation

Now for accommodation you'll start off in the backpackers. It is pretty good living in the backpackers. I used to live in the backpackers in Hong Kong, then in Guangzhou. In Hong Kong a lot of people living in the backpackers were permanent. It was cheap, central and they had a kitchen and a fridge so you could cook. In Hanoi because it is a major backpacker stop over point, there are backpackers coming and going all the time. In the backpackers where I lived there were only three of us semi permanents in the building. Another teacher and a guy that lived off the internet. And we got on quite well together. The rest of the travellers were just coming and going, and some travellers were always coming back so you saw some of them three times over the period of a month.

In Hanoi there are three different prices for hostels. The cheapest was $3.50 US a night and it was value for money. They had free beer after 6 pm until you got sick of it. There was a keg in the corner and you just helped yourself. This suited me because I could still get a free beer after I got home from class. This was very basic and you got what you paid for. There was even a free breakfast thrown in. Every place has a free breakfast. And the staff were exceptionally friendly and helpful. Another hostel I stayed at was only $4 US per night and it was centrally located. It was in a really good spot. But the staff were not very friendly so I shifted out after a while. The first hostel I stayed in was a $7 a night party hostel and it was excellent, but I had to shift out as I was getting drunk every night. They started the free beer at 4 pm, so if I wasn't doing anything I was pretty wasted. There are hotels and hostels everywhere, so you don't really need to book one online. And if you don't like the hostel move next door.

A new hostel sprang up right next to the cathedral, and at the moment as of writing, it is the place to live. This place had the three things I looked for. A place to hang up my washing in the sun, like on the balcony or on the roof. A lot of places do not do this, and with being a teacher in the summer you live in sweat. So after class when I got home I would wash out the sweat and hang up my clothes to dry overnight. In the rainy season you had to be careful, as sudden tropical downpours can pop up out of nowhere, and if you didn't have your clothes pegged down they would blow away. Sometimes in the morning you would come out and your clothes would be soaked. That was number one thing I wanted, and if the hostel didn't have a place to hang up clothes I would not stay there.

What I Wanted In A Hostel

In Vietnam a whole industry has sprung up washing clothes, so for 1500 to 2000 dong you can get your clothes washed and dried. In some cases it was a lucky dip getting all your clothes back. Sometimes you end up with somebody else's. And some of the time your clothes are not even washed they are just rinsed and you get them back. It sounds good but if you are a teacher you can use two shirts and pants a day. And I usually go out for a run around Hoan Kiem Lake in the mornings, so I would come back covered in sweat and I just like to rinse the sweat off my clothes. For me having a place to hang out clothes was very important, and not many hostels have a clothes line available. In China most have a place to hang out clothes. When one hostel said I couldn't hang my clothes on the balcony any more I left. That is how important it is to me.

Also I always looked for hot water so I could drink tea all day. And if they had cold water, so I could full up my water bottle that was a plus. A lot of places just had hot water during breakfast time, so I would fill up my flask then. Also most schools had water on tap, so I used to fill up my water bottles and hot water flask at school. But if the hostel had hot and cold water on tap it was a plus. So throw a thermos, a cup and a good water bottle in your backpack, because you are going to need them.

These two things were what I wanted, so I always asked for them and if they didn't have them I moved on. The third thing I liked was a place to use my laptop. All hostels had free wifi, but not all had a place where you could sit down and just play around on the laptop. The $4 hostel was the best but the staff got the better of me. The guy on reception I'm sure would make the village idiot look intelligent, or he just had it in for me. In Vietnam the hotels keep your passport, that is the law, and I needed my passport to go to the bank, and he wouldn't give it to me so in the end I only talked to the night staff. They hadn't mastered the art of being nice to customers, but that hostel had everything I needed. I put up with it for a month and then moved on. The cleaning lady used to walk around with the radio on her phone blaring out Vietnam songs, and she would sleep on the bunks in the dorm with the radio blaring away. And I am sure she took my soap. I got the impression a lot of businesses do not like us foreigners. It is a sort of love hate relationship. They need us so they can rip us off, but they hate us at the same time. You will get that feeling of contempt when you are there. And I am not surprised as the Hoan Kiem area is usually crawling with foreigners. Even in the middle of summer when the temperature is hovering around 40 degrees C, there are foreigners walking round.

Actually if you can find a homestay that doesn't work you to death then that is the way to go. I have lived in 2 different homestays and I only worked one hour teaching a day in the morning and I got a free bed in a dorm and at night we all had a meal together. My friend lived in a different homestay where he worked 5 hours a week at the homestay and then they sent him out to teach at other schools for the going rate. That is the best deal I have heard of and he had a room to himself. I think he is still there. So if you are still learning to teach and need a bit of confidence then finding a good homestay is the way to go. Now be careful as some homestays want you to work 3 hours a day and you live in a dorm with food. You are always surrounded by students so you have instant friends and they will take you anywhere you want to go, https://www.facebook.com /ielhomestayshanoi/ I Stayed here they are good

https://www.workaway.info/en/destination/asia/vn here is a list of homestays

https://hippohelp.com/ is quite a good place to find homestays

An Example Of Getting Ripped OFF

I take vitamins all the time so when I got food poisoning I went and brought some Vitamin C. You can buy a little blister packet with 10 pills in it. The first shop charged me 20,000 dong which is just under $1 U.S. I had no idea what the price should be so I brought it. When I ran out I went to another shop and brought the same packet plus a blister pack of Magnesium and both together cost 20,000 dong so I asked how much and the Vitamin C was and it was 5,000 dong. That is when I realised I had been screwed. Anyway when I ran out this time I went to another shop and the price for both the Vit C and the Magnesium came to 55,000 dong for both so I walked out. The shop assistant could see I had brought the same pills before as I showed her the empty blister packets, and she slapped on her commission. To some people you are just a milk cow. Anyway in the little shop by the cafe, the price for both the Vitamin C and the magnesium came to 19,000 dong, and the Vitamin C was 4,000 dong, so she had a customer for life. Now that is what you are up against.

This is not an extreme example, it happens all the time. Another price difference is the adapter for the Vietnam socket. In the supermarket I paid 15,000 dong, while on the street from the street vendors and in the electronic shops the price was 60,000 dong.

You Need A Phone Number

Also there are some shops breaking the mould like the VinMart, a Vietnam 7/11 equivalent from the biggest company in Vietnam. There prices are very reasonable as are most of the supermarkets. Also if you are after phones or any phone related stuff there are only 2 places to go Vittel and thegioididong.com. The Gioididong are the black and yellow sign frontage shops scattered around the city, and Vittel are the blue shop frontages. And in the Gioididong shop in Hoan Kiem they speak English. My phone crapped out, so I went in there and they got it up and running again, and they didn't charge anything. So I topped it up there.

Anyway with the phone companies I used Mobiphone but I will not recommend them. The first month was good, but after I topped up for 70,000 dong it lasted about 4 days and I did this 3 times so I stopped topping it up. Now I don't know if that was me or Mobiphone, but a number of foreigners did not like Mobiphone so it is up to you, but I would try something else. I heard good things about the Vittel shops from other foreigners so you could also try them out. Also don't buy the top up cards from the vendors for 100,000 dong, as they can give you anything and I ended up with a promotion card that cost 100,000 dong and was basically useless. I now use Vinaphone and have no problems

Anyway back to the hostel next to the church. They have mastered the art of being nice to the backpackers and they are. At the moment there is no feeling of contempt at all in that hostel, or a few of the other popular hostels. This hostel is one of the few I recommend, so if you are in Hanoi check it out. The only problem is they cram you in the dorms, but the beds are curtained off so you have your own space.

The big church is something else, it is crowded at all masses, and there is some guy turning you away if you are not properly dressed. Someone forgot to tell him that churches around the Western World are having problems getting people to come inside. I was turned away as I was wearing a singlet and shorts and you are not allowed to show your shoulders. A lot of people get turned away. Quite sad really. I go to church every Sunday and we can't get enough people in our church, and here they are turning them away.

Eating Out In Hanoi

As most hostels do not have a kitchen, you are at the mercy of the street food merchants, and or little restaurants. Some are good, some are not so good, and some screw you to the wall. Also it can depend on the waitress. For street food, you just sit down, they give you a bowl of food and you eat it, then you pay for it. Street food price range is usually 20,000 dong for the cheapest to around 50,000 dong for a dish with lots of meat.

There is one dish I call the worst food in the world and it is "shrimp paste". Here you get a dish of chopped up dofu, bean curd or whatever it is called, and a little bowl of yucky brown paste. You are supposed to dip the dofu in the little bowl of yucky brown stuff and eat it. If you like something that tastes really terrible you'll love this stuff, but if you are like me you wont. You know you are about to eat this stuff as the whole restaurant will be looking at you. The only time I tried this, I wondered why everybody was looking at me, and after I took my first mouthful I understood why.

I ended up eating mostly at a type of buffet style place. The restaurant has a glass covered display case and in the case there are many different dishes of food. The prices are usually 20K, 25K and 30K. I used to say 25K and then start pointing to what I wanted. And when I had 25K worth of food they would stop. Some tried to pile the food on, so they could charge you more, while others were very reasonable. There were some that were very unreasonable, and those were the ones you didn't go back to.

After a while you will have your round of restaurants that you go to, and if they like you they will give you more. I think it pays to be a regular customer as they get to know you after a while. Really in these types of small restaurants there is a steady stream of customers, so they are not short of a customer or two, therefore they do not need to be nice to you.

Most hostels have free breakfast but it is not much, so I used to add to it. Like I would take an avocado or a small tin of sardines as well as some extra bread. You could buy these at the supermarket. Also I would take my own salt, as the food was not salty enough for me. In the heat as you are sweating all the time, you do need salt.

Just one thing to be very careful of is they love MSG. The longest aisle in the supermarket is MSG and all the food you buy anywhere has MSG in it so be careful. I lived in the homestay so I could cook but I usually lived off coconuts, sugar cane drink and lots of fruit and tins of small fish. Bread is really good here so I could always make a sandwich.

Moving Out Of The Dorm

At $5 US dollars a night you are paying $150 a month and that is less than the price of a room in a shared house. So if you like you can start looking for a room. I preferred the backpackers, as there was a steady stream of people moving through, and inter spaced between these were the permanents. And as I said before "instant friends" are around you all the time, and you can have a really good time living in a backpackers. You usually never have to eat alone.

Now if you wanted to rent something, you would usually end up in a share house, where you would rent a room for a minimum of $150 US, usually around $200 for a fully contained room with bed, fridge, desk and chairs as well as an air conditioner and unlimited internet and you paid your electricity on the meter. I preferred to pay the lump sum, as some people love air conditioning and that usually cranked up the electricity bill, especially in summer. Be careful sharing electricity I preferred having the meter. Most places were furnished so everything was supplied, and you got a maid to keep it clean and keep an eye on you. I was told by local Vietnamese people I could get something a lot cheaper but it would be in an old building. I never followed it up so I don't know.

You could pick up a studio apartment, self contained for around $350 US + amenities. But why live by yourself. Now if you are going to do this you need to have a reasonable income coming in so you are not scratching for a living. Anyway I prefer to live around people so I liked staying at the backpackers. And living here applying for jobs, going for an interview and hearing nothing back, can be quite taxing on your psychic. But there is a plus, you soon learn how to get around this city using buses and Grab. Also it is a never ending grind getting teaching hours, so you have to keep doing it. Even if you have enough classes, you still have to keep an eye on the job sites to see what is out there.

Where To Look For A Room

In Vietnam everything is facebook so check out the sites on facebook and expat.com usually has some good houses available. Actually they are not in order of date so keep an eye on the date. You must check how long you have to pay the rent. Some say every three months with one month deposit and some say six months, so check it out as this varies. So make sure you know what you are getting yourself into. The lower end of the scale is around $150 US plus some amenities. There are cheaper but they are a long way from the city centre. The other thing you have to check is location, as in some cases like most of them you need a motorcycle to get to the apartment. If you use the buses check out where the closest bus stop is. If you use Grab, see how long it takes them to get there. So have a read of some of the advertisements and decide if you want to get out of the dorm.

The main problem in the hotel is no kitchen. If I could find a dorm with a kitchen that was reasonably priced I would stay there. If you are really interested in getting out of a dorm you can pick up a hotel room for yourself, minimum $200 US if you pay monthly. But you have to ask around and they are usually word of mouth. On the Massive website you will sometimes see advertisements for rooms or houses for rent. You can pick up a cheap place, but the owner would like a 6 month contract, and if you want less the price goes up. And a lot of owners and agents try not to give you a fixed price. There is always some expenses they like to add on, like one agent wanted to add on cutting the trees as an added expense.

There are a number of Hanoi Massive websites. Hanoi Massive Jobs https://www.facebook.com/groups/hanoimassivejobs and just Hanoi Massive https://www.facebook.com/groups/138 0006002 15676/ which is a site for what is happening in Hanoi and sometimes you see rooms advertised on this site. Another Facebook Site to look at is Hanoi Comrades https://www .facebook.com/groups/581773388574145/ another what's happening in Hanoi site which sometimes has advertisements for rooms for rent.

There are facebook sites for nearly everything so play around on search on facebook and see what pops up. There is a new Massive site https://www.facebook.com/groups/1682171775381397/

for renting a room or flat but it has already been invaded by the companies selling houses. Another site to look at is expat.com. Sign into the alerts on the site for Hanoi and every now and then you will get an email when one is available. Now this site does not overload your email box so it is good, and the prices are very reasonable. Sometimes way out of town you can pick up a room for under $100 a month. For foreigners all the rooms are furnished. If you get a cheap room from a local friend you will have to find the furniture, so paying the higher price pays off in the end. We looked at a few rooms for locals but they were all unfurnished so we let them go. They were a bit cheaper but not much.

Also a lot of owners and or agents want a long rental like 6 months, and if you want a shorter time the price goes up. I checked out one room way out of town that was advertised for $64 a month but ended up closer to $100 a month after everything was included. Now living away from Hoan Kiem the city centre is a lot cheaper. Food and coffee and everything in the markets is cheaper so if you don't want or need to live in the city centre try the outer suburbs. The rent is a bit cheaper and nearly everything is a bit cheaper and they don't have the milk cow mentality, so it is more enjoyable living there.

Anyway I needed some privacy so I got out of the dorm. I stayed here, amazing place https://www.facebook.com/room. of.old quarter/ I'm very lucky I found this place, the small room is $144 and the big room $168 with a deposit of 3.5 million dong and they had everything I needed. Mind you the first electric jug they gave me nearly caught fire but we sorted that out. And the toilet door is suspect I nearly locked myself in the shower, but I managed to get the door open without wrecking the place. The biggest surprise was the toilet is just sitting on the floor so if you over lean one way the whole thing could end up on the floor. But other than all these it is a good place. I got this off the http://www.expat.com/en /housing/asia/vietnam/hanoi/ and I get to pay every month.

Back To Teaching

With teaching you do not need to have any teaching aids or anything, the school will give you a teaching plan and everything you need in class. On the lesson plan they even say what games to do. If you have a game you want to try, tell your assistant and they will arrange it for you. All you need to do is get to class on time and be creative. Hopefully you can do that. If you are not reliable, and do not find a substitute teacher when you cannot take a class, you will lose your job and that is it. Most schools are small and do not have any backup teachers, so if you don't find a teacher for your class the students miss out and the schools don't like that.

I think the teaching situation evolved around backpackers as teachers. The school supplies everything and you just have to roll up and take the class. I think that is why there is such a high turnover rate of foreigners as teachers. The schools don't expect you to stay and they know you have to leave the country every three months, so they expect you to go. Also you can only love this city for so long. Most food places are honest and don't rip you off. Taxis and motorbike taxis are a different story so I use Grab whenever I can. But the constant grind of living in a very crowded city with very narrow streets, tends to get you down, or me anyway, after a while. So I can see why there is a high turnover of teachers. So keep applying to schools that you have already sent your CV too if they keep advertising. Also keep an eye on Massive Jobs so you can put an advertisement on the site when you have to do a visa run.

I think one of the main reasons people leave is they just can't get enough hours each week to survive. In the English centres if you are lucky you get three hours teaching a night but most likely you will end up with one and a half hours and more hours on the weekend. If you work for a company school you will end up with more hours and therefore more money but they usually want a one year contract. If you work in the public school system you will end up going from school to school but only during the school year. Then during summer you will end up with summer school and that can be quite lucrative but very tiring especially in 35 degree heat. Here teachers come and go all the time and it is up to you how long you stay here, but there is a community of permanent teachers if you stay long term. I keep bumping into teachers I met years ago

Finding A Bank

Getting a bank account is usually not a problem, but in some banks it can be according to other teachers. I got an account at the Agriculture Bank or AgriBank and had no problem. It takes a week to get a bank card, and with this bank I could not find too many ATMs for this bank. For most banks to withdraw money from the machine you pay a fee of 40,000 dong, and to withdraw money from your credit card costs over 100,000 dong, so use your debit card. Also there is a limit of so many million dong a day but I never went over the limit so I don't know what it is.

Also all banks advertise an interest rate of over 6% but you can only get that for the length of your visa and the normal interest rate is 1%. I tried to put some money in the high interest rate but I didn't have enough time on my visa. When Vietnam banks allow foreigners to put money on the high interest rate I'll put as much as I can and leave it sit there for 10 years and it should nearly double. The Vietnam economy looks good and I think it will still be around for the future. They are not doing a mad scramble to modernize like China did. I think they will slow down. It is a generational thing China was a rip off place about 20 years ago now it is good. Vietnam is a rip off place so it will take time for the mentality to change.

Leaving

Now leaving Hanoi on the bus to Nanning China. The whole leaving Hanoi on the bus has changed recently. The Hanoi NanMing bus station at the Ben Xe Khach Luong Yen bus station has closed, and that changes everything. Now the best way is to get your hotel to buy you a ticket, and they go for around 600,000 dong. And the little limousine bus will pick you up, and if there is not too many people on the bus you ride in style to the border.

Now the border is all modern new buildings so getting stamped out of Vietnam and stamped into China is no problem. Before you can buy a ticket for the bus you need a valid Chinese Visa in your passport. The bus from the border to Nanning left the border bus station at 1.30, and we arrived at the LangDong main bus station around the corner from the Nanning train station just after 4.30 pm. And if your backpack is not too heavy you are in for a good 20 minutes walk to the hostel on JieFang Street. A taxi costs around 10RMB.

And that is the end of your teaching experience in Hanoi. Nanning has one serious problem and that is it is a beautiful city where you don't get ripped off everywhere. And the water in the river is so clean people swim in it. The more I stayed there, the more I fell in love with the city so on my next trip I will stay longer in Nanning. Might even look for a job.

Things You Need For Hanoi

Towel as a number of hostels do not supply a towel. You can rent one but you have to hide it from the cleaning lady or she will take it and hand it back.

Unbreakable cup so the cleaning lady can't break it.

Toilet bag for your toothbrush, soap and whatever so the cleaning lady can't help herself to your soap.

You do not need to bring an Adapter for your phone and laptop, as you can buy one at the Intermex Supermarket in Hoan Kiem for around 12,000 to 15,000 dong. Mine mysteriously went missing but I don't think it was the cleaning lady, not this time anyway.

A few clothes, as things are cheap here but not as cheap as China.

A good pair of flip flops for your feet. My cheap Chinese flip flops lasted about a week so you need a few good pairs.

Old sandals and shoes you need repaired, there are some very good shoe repairers on the street. The one I liked was between the Cathedral and the old Hoan Kiem Library.

For teaching adults - long pants and black leather shoes plus good clean shirts.

For kids - T-shirt and shorts and sandals or flip flops as you have to take your shoes off before you go inside a kindergarten.

I would add a small knife set. A good blunt knife for making a sandwich in the park. A pocket knife should be OK.

A few light weight teaching aids like your favourite flash cards.

Time Line For Getting A Job

Before You Leave:

Check out the websites listed in this book

Check hostels

Look at school advertisements.

Check out a map of Hanoi or the cities you want to go to.

Load up your phone with all the apps you need and learn how to use them, especially Google translate and a currency converter.

Get some business cards printed – Vistaprint is pretty good. In Hanoi I still don't know where to get business cards printed.

If you think you need one, get a ESL teaching certificate. Most jobs ask for one.

When You Get There:

Put Hanoi on Google maps

Find a reasonable priced hostel

Get a phone number – you need that to get a job.

Tell everybody you are a teacher looking for a job.

Download the Grab app to your phone and start using it

Start using the buses so you can get used to them.

Or rent or buy a bike and learn your way around the city.

Start sending you CV to advertised jobs. I used to apply for any job that I could get to and I could do usually about 2 to 3 a day.

Do this everyday until you have enough hours to live and save.

Give your CV or business card to any school near where you live.

A Breakdown Of What I Did

I sent my CV to 49 different advertisements

including 5 fill in classes

I received 28 replies back

I was invited for 9 interview/demo classes

I turned down 3 that didn't suit me

and I started work for 4 different schools

One was a company school that paid monthly – 2 and a ½ hours a class

Two were home schools in peoples houses, they paid after class - 1 and a ½ hours a class

The last one was a small English school, paid after class - 1 and a ½ hours a class

I received 4 offers of fill in classes but I couldn't do them as I was busy – these were schools who texted me when they needed a teacher not when I applied.

I picked up 3 fill in classes

Now I don't know if you will have to apply for that many jobs. They were all city jobs and they were all part time.

Summary Time

When you go into Vietnam especially Hanoi, you are going back 20 to 40 years and that includes the rip off mentality. Out of the big cities the rip off mentality is not so bad. Get used to it, it is a part of life.

Hostels are plentiful and everywhere. You need to find one that suits your needs and that could mean living in one until you do.

Get a phone number, I recommend Vittel or the Gioididong shop and vinaphone

Tell everybody you are a teacher looking for a job.

Check out the apps on your phone so you know how to use them.

There are new jobs advertised everyday, so start sending in your CV as soon as possible. Make sure you have photos and videos from other classes, to show the school you know what you are doing.

To start work as soon as possible get an agent. They will get you in front of a classroom faster than you can. Hand your CV in person to the schools near where you live. There are schools everywhere.

While waiting for a job get to know the city. Try out Grab and the buses or buy or rent a bike and find your way around the city.

Start eating on the street.

Vietnam is a good place to stop and teach.

Have a great time.

How I Got To Hanoi

Lowu is still the same, it hasn't changed much over the years. Anyway after you come out of the border control building into Shenzhen, you keep walking straight ahead to get to the train station. There it is, pretty straight forward. Chinese Nationals can book their tickets at the automatic windows, but we have to line up at the ticket windows, and buy a ticket. You need your passport. Anyway the train ticket and getting on the train is idiot proof. As soon as your train number shows up on the screen, there is a mad rush for the gate, and you just follow the crowd to the platform. The ticket is very straight forward, find your carriage then find your seat. If anyone is sitting in your seat, show them your ticket and they will usually move. They are possibly from an earlier or later train. The trains usually leave every 15 minutes. Now you have just entered the 21 st century. As soon as you get out of Shenzhen, you are travelling along at 160kms/hour. Welcome to China. After your train from Shenzhen stops at Tian He Dong, you are in Mainstream China.

Find your way out, and head into the subway which is on the left, after you walk out of the high speed train section. It is pretty idiot proof, as long as you know where you are going. If you book your hotel before you get there, you should know where to get off the subway. On the subway they have their own version of the TSA, but they don't grope you. They just rub the detectors over your bag.

If you get your China visa in Hong Kong, the price was $600HK for a double entry visa, you have to wait 3 days to pick it up. How long you get to stay in China usually depends on the visa. I ended up being allowed to stay in China for 30 days. So check your visa to make sure you know how long you are allowed to stay in China. Don't overstay it is a 5000RMB yuan fine for overstaying. It could actually be 5000 yuan a day. I'm not to sure about that. Just don't overstay. I got my Vietnam visa in Guangzhou at the visa office in the Landmark Hotel. It was another 3 day wait and another 600RMB this time. But Guangzhou is an amazing city.

China And Google

There is one seriously big problem with China and that is, they are extremely paranoid. So normal internet stuff we take for granted is not available in China, like facebook, youtube and google. Missing out on facebook and youtube is not really all that bad. Make sure you put an unblocked on your computer and mobile before you go to China, because most of the usual unblocker sites are blocked. I use ultrasurf and that is free and pretty good. You must put the unblocker on your computer and mobile phone before you enter China. All the unblocker sites are blocked in China. But then again somebody at the hostel should be able to drop it on your phone. I can get gmail, facebook and youtube no problem. So you can get by that slight hassle, not a problem. In some of the net bars unblockers just don't work at all. They work in McDonalds. There is one major serious problem with google being blocked, and that is Google Play. Buying a smart phone in China, might not be a very smart thing to do, because the phones have Google Play in Chinese, so that means you could be stuffed from day one. You will find Google Play under the apps which are all in Chinese. On the phones you can change a lot of things into English or your home language, but all the app instructions are in Chinese. And I couldn't work out how to change that into English. The apps in Chinese is not really a problem, because the youth hostels in China are full of young people, and they will help you load any app you want, including Google Play. But since Google Play doesn't work in China, you may as well load it just before you leave. I wouldn't recommend loading Google Play until you leave, as some apps need Google Play to work, and Google doesn't work in China. If you download Google Play while in China, nothing happens when you click the

Google Store Button. All the app instructions for the Chinese apps, are in Chinese, and you do need things like a map and a translator, as well as a currency converter. If you get somebody in the hostel to help you, they might be able to change the language to English. Some of the young Chinese people are very tech savvy.

There are other ways to get past this Google Play problem, but you need to be very tech savvy. First you have to root your phone, then you can download Google Play. Check out these sites here, they seem to know what they are talking about, when it comes to rooting a phone. http://www.kingoapp.com It can be done but it is a hassle. https://www.oneclickroot.com/rootable/ And rooting the latest Android, like 5.1 is not as easy as rooting 5.0. https://www.imyfone.com/android-root-tips/root-android-5-1-1/ Keep that in mind. There are tech savvy people in China, who can put Google Play on your phone, but find one before you buy a phone. http://www.digitaltrends.com/mobile/how-to-root-android/2/ If your guy is really tech savvy, he or she should be able to set your phone up, so it is the same as a phone brought overseas. Or you can do it yourself. This thread here shows you how to do it http://forum.xda-developers.com/showthread.php?t=18 74285. Because with the Chinese phone, there are still a lot of pages in Chinese, even after you change the language to English. All the apps are still in Chinese. Anyway the price of phones is very similar to the price overseas, so they are not that much cheaper. The best bet is to take a reasonable cheap and good phone with you. Because after you have found somebody to root it, and change everything into English it could be more expensive. Also thieves are a bit of a problem, so don't take the latest Galaxy 7 into South East Asia, as you might not have it when you leave. The biggest problem with getting your phone stolen is, if you live off GPS to find your way back to your hotel, you could have one serious problem finding your hotel.

Electric Bike Capital Of The World

If you want to play around in China for a bit, you can take the high speed train from Guangzhou South Station to Nanning, where you can catch the night train to Hanoi. And you can stop off in Guilin and Yangshao for a look around there. It is well worth it. Anyway the train for Hanoi leaves around 6 in the evening, so you can either get to Nanning in the afternoon, or you can spend a bit of time exploring the city. Now Nanning is the undisputed electric bike capital of the planet. And there are electric bikes everywhere, and they are trying to sell them nearly everywhere too. And for a little over 2000 RMB yuan plus on road costs, which I have no idea how much they are. But they should include a couple of helmets and a very strong lock, then you could be the proud owner of your very own electric bike. And join the millions of other bike riders in Nanning. Now Nanning is very well controlled, the bikes all stop at red lights, and when you are crossing the road you walk past about 20 bikes stopped for the red light. And behind them the line of bikes snakes off into the pollution. When the lights turn green the bikes take off and go in all directions, and when the light turns red they all stop. Utterly amazing. After you get to Hanoi you will understand.

Nanning is a really nice city, not too big or not to small. If you want to stay in Nanning, which I recommend, stay at the hostel at 3 JieFang Street off RenMin Zhong. For this hostel it pays to get a reservation as it is very popular. Nanning is an amazing place, and when you get to Hanoi you will understand why. You need to get the bus number 7 from the new station to the old station, and the buses are not too crowded. Even the buses in Guangzhou now are not too crowded. Guangzhou relies on the subway now and that can be very crowded. Also traffic jams are a part of life in the big cities, but with the subway there are no jams.

Trains And The Modern High Speed Train Stations

Now to find your way to Nanning, you need to get to the South Railway Station in Guangzhou, at the end of the number 2 blue subway line. I went early in the morning, before the rush but it was still crowded. Anyway when you get to the station, you can't really follow the crowd, as most of the people are there for the first time, and they don't know where to go either. I followed the English sign for Concourse and in the distance I could see crowds of people. Now this station is huge, I mean really huge, so expect to do some serious walking. Now after you get back to the crowds you have to start looking for the ticket office. Now the Chinese people can buy tickets from the automatic ticket machines, but you have to find the ticket office. And that can be quite daunting, as the ticket office is actually outside. Anyway the girl at the window spoke English so it was no problem. But she only gave me half an hour to find the train I needed. Of course I was doing some serious panicking, but didn't need too. All you have to do is, get on the escalator going up and you end up where you should be. Then you just check the departures board, to find out which gate you need to go to. Also on the top right hand corner of the ticket, is a number like 11B and that is the gate you should head for. Didn't need to panic, got there with 20 minutes to spare. Idiot proof to the max. Then the gates open. You put your ticket in the slot, pull it out the top, and the gate opens and you go down the escalator to the platform, and jump on the train. This train can reach speeds of up to and over 300kms per hour, this one didn't but it was still a very fast train.

The fast trains are cheaper, faster and safer than the intercity buses, and you are way into the 21st century, not still stuck in the 20th century like you will be when you get to Hanoi. On the intercity buses in China, they show live scenes from the security cameras on the buses, of bus crashes to help you put on your seat belt. This type of stuff would never been shown in the west, but they do blank out the faces. In some crashes it is amazing anybody survived.

Because I left early I got to Nanning early, took the number 7 bus to the local train station and hang out in Nanning. The local train station was the exact opposite of the modern new station. To get in you had to show your passport, and then the TSA lady rubbed you down and felt your pockets. You had to stand on a special stool and turn around so she could do both sides. All train stations do this, so get used to it.

A Cheaper Ticket To Hanoi

Now I was in for a bit of a surprise here as the computer for the train was down, and an enterprising young Chinese couple were booking us all in as a tour, so we all got cheap seats. There was 12 all together in our party, and that was the start of one of the best train trips I've ever been on. It was one of these instant friend situations. We all got on well together, Chinese, Vietnamese, Japanese and me. And after we got to Hanoi we dispersed and never saw each other again.

Nanning Railway station was very organized for a small station. The English speaking window is window Number 1. It used to be Number 16, but now it is Number One, and the women actually spoke good English. Anyway, after the Chinese couple had sorted out the tickets, we had about 4 hours to spare to wonder around the city. So I dropped my backpack off at the left luggage and headed out into the wide world of Nanning. Another amazing Chinese city.

The night train was incredible, we all had bunks and we were all together. China is modern and organized, so when you cross the border you are going back to 1940 in nearly everything, including bribing border guards. It was a good trip, They woke us up to go through the border controls, and we changed some money, and then it was back to sleep till we got to Hanoi.

Now that is one way to get here. The other way is to fly. Now when you fly into Vietnam you need to get a Visa On Arrival letter and the easiest way is online. You pay for the service fee online, and then at the airport you cough up around $25US dollars or equivalent for the visa. You can also go to the embassy and get a visa from there if you like. You must have a visa or an online Visa On Arrival hard copy, because they will not let you on the plane without one.

If You Like My Book

Please write a review on Amazon showing your appreciation

How to Write a Review on Amazon

Go to https://www.amazon.com/dp/B083BVZB1Z

- Scroll down to Customer Reviews

- Click on "Write a customer review" and do your thing. As long or as short as you like.

Amazon will then check it and after a while it will be live on Amazon.

Now you can give the book a grade, how many Gold Stars would you like to give the book.

Thank you

Peter LeGrove

Other Books By Peter LeGrove

Teach and Travel in China

This little book is all about going to China and getting a job teaching English. Even though it is Guangzhou specific it still covers little things that could happen in China. A good read if you are heading out into the world to travel.

How To Teach Young Learners ESL

This book is an accumulation of my seven years of classroom teaching, face to face with kids from kindergarten to the end of primary school. This is what worked for me, and it has been distilled from lots of stuff that didn't work. So you end up with the crème de la crème. Teaching kids is the way to go, if you are into teaching and traveling.

Reading Student Struggling Student

If you are not into leaving your child in front of the computer to learn to read, then this book is for you. This is a hands on approach to teaching your child to read, using a method that has been teaching children to read for over a hundred years. And it is still applicable in this internet age.

How To Add Qualifications To Your CV Using FREE Courses

To add more color to your CV, and to help give you the edge in the job market. Fill up the spaces with certificates from free courses run by world renowned universities. There is a whole new world of free education out there in cyberspace, you just have to plug into and this little book shows you where it all is.

How To Make An Online CV Using Free Software

With the internet taking over our lives it is only a matter of time before you apply for an online job using an Online CV. In this little book you will learn how to put together a professional Online CV using only FREE software freely available over the internet. Also what you learn can be adapted to online presentations as well.

Prepare Your Children For The Future NOW

The world with the internet is changing so fast now it is very difficult to keep up. So to keep your children ahead of the curve you need to start them early on the internet. This way when they are ready to head out into the New World of cyberspace they are already over half way there.

Live Cheap In An UnCheap World

For some reason the world we live in is getting more and more expensive, so now it is time to change. To make your money last longer, you either have to tighten your belt, make more money or do things differently. Now this little books shows you ways to do all three so you can end up with more money at the end of the week.

Prepare Now To Survive Mother Nature's Wrath Or Mankind's Madness

At present in the world, there is a group of people who think the world is heading for a major collapse. And on the other side, there has been an increase in what Mother Nature can do to the planet. This book is about common sense preparing for what could happen without going overboard.

Thank you and all the best on your journey into teaching English in Vietnam. Just remember it takes a bit of planning and then you are ready to head into South East Asia to give it all you got.

Peter Legrove